Liquid or Solid?

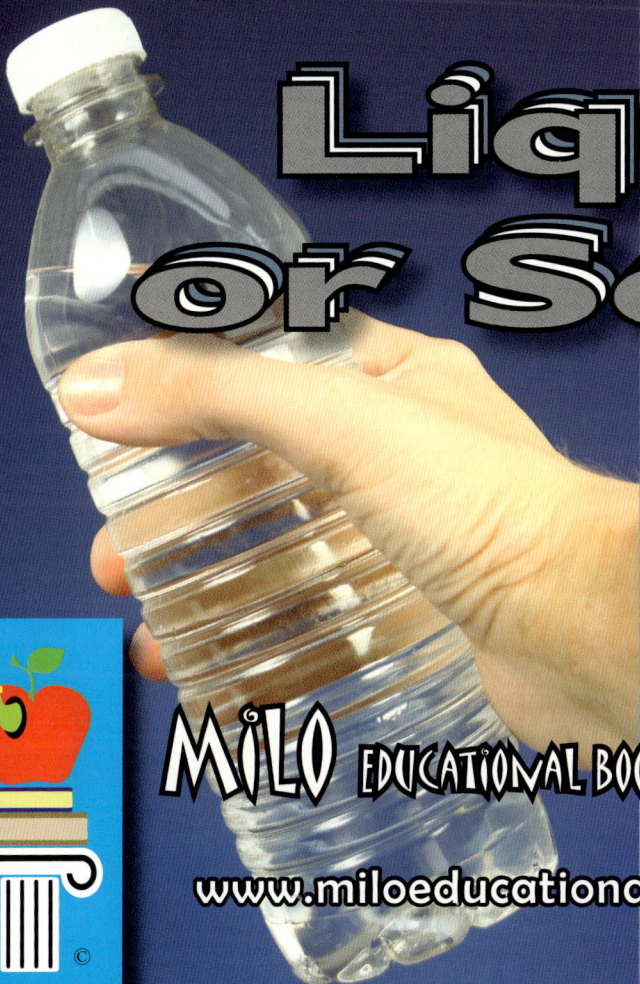

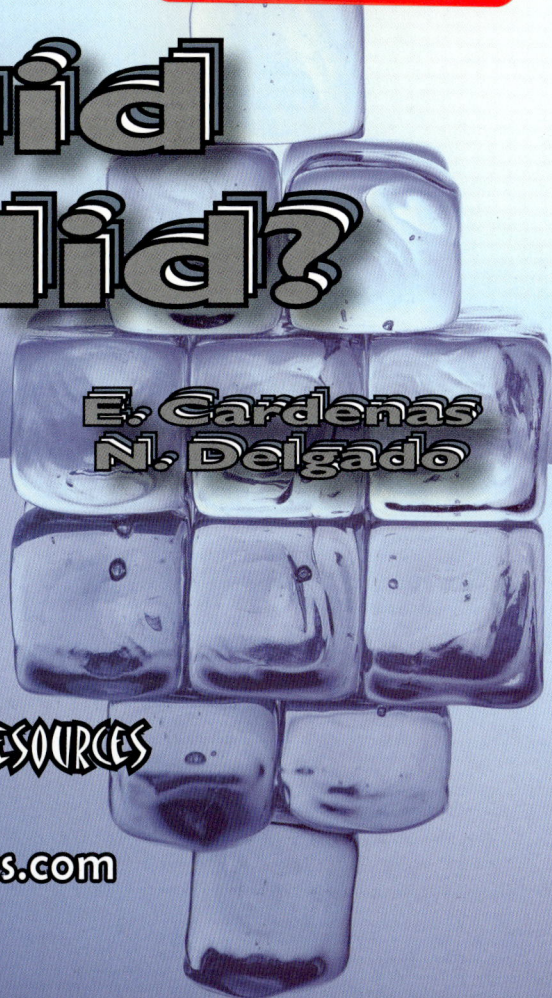

E. Cardenas
N. Delgado

MiLO EDUCATIONAL BOOKS & RESOURCES

www.miloeducationalbooks.com

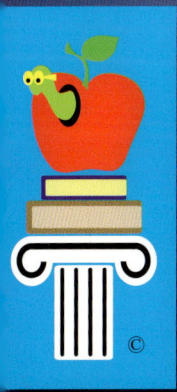

Published by:

MILO EDUCATIONAL BOOKS & RESOURCES

www.miloeducationalbooks.com
P.O. Box 41353, Houston, Texas 77241-1353
Phone: (888) 640-MILO & (713) 466-MILO
Fax: (888) 641-MILO & (713) 896-MILO

Liquid or Solid? written by E. Cardenas & N. Delgado

ISBN-13:   978-1-60698-039-2   Paperback
                978-1-60698-040-8   Six-pack paperback
                978-1-60698-041-5   Big book paperback

Library of Congress Control Number: 2008905752

First Edition

Printed in China

Visit our website at **www.miloeducationalbooks.com** for more information and resources for students, teachers, and parents.

Credits:

Front cover & page 1: © 2006 Dana Heinemann (left) & Michal Herman (right)/ShutterStock, Inc.; Back cover: © 2006 Stephen Coburn/ShutterStock, Inc.; Page 3: © 2006 Cathleen Clapper/ShutterStock, Inc.; Page 4: © 2006 Tina Rencelj/ShutterStock, Inc.; Page 5: © 2006 Marcelo Pinheiro/ShutterStock, Inc.; Page 6: © 2006 Elke Dennis/ShutterStock, Inc.; Page 7: © 2006 Teo Boon Keng Alvin/ShutterStock, Inc.; Page 8: © 2006 Elena Elisseeva/ShutterStock, Inc.; Page 9: © 2006 Vilmos Varga/ShutterStock, Inc.; Page 10: © 2006 Magdalena Kucova/ShutterStock, Inc.; Page 11: © 2006 Olga Shelego/ShutterStock, Inc.; Page 12: © 2006 Edyta Pawlowska/ShutterStock, Inc.; Page 13: © 2006 Lana Langlois/ShutterStock, Inc.; Page 14: © 2006 Rodolfo Arpia/ShutterStock, Inc.; Page 15: © 2006 Edgars Dubrovskis/ShutterStock, Inc.; Page 16 from left to right & top to bottom: © 2006 Scott Hampton, Radu Razvan, Monika Adamczyk & Artur Bogacki/ShutterStock, Inc.

A liquid takes the form of the container that holds it.

A solid has a defined shape.

What is a liquid?
What is a solid?

Milk is a liquid.

An ice pop is a solid.

Lemonade is a liquid.

A lemon is a solid.

Juice is a liquid.

An orange is a solid.

9

Tea is a liquid.

A leaf is a solid.

A milkshake is a liquid.

A strawberry is a solid.

Hot cocoa is a liquid.

A chocolate bar is a solid.

Now look at
the pictures.
What is a liquid?
What is a solid?